Fool for
Thought

Reflections on Life, Identity, and Open-Mindedness

David Vega

Praise for *Fool for Thought*

"If you have ever failed, doubted, or started over, this book is for you. David Vega reminds us that wisdom is earned, and the future still looks bright."

—**Patrick Bet-David**, Author, Entrepreneur, CEO of Valuetainment

"*Fool for Thought* isn't filled with ego or empty motivation— it's a sincere, reflective journey from someone who's been in the trenches. David Vega writes with humility, character, and clarity. His words invite you to pause, reflect, and ask the questions that matter. In a world of noise, this book offers the kind of wisdom we need more of."

—**Lieutenant General Leroy Sisco, USA (Ret.)**

"In a world flooded with noise, *Fool for Thought* is a rare signal—authentic, introspective, and deeply moving. David Vega doesn't just share stories; he invites readers into a journey of purpose, faith, and courageous self-reflection. As someone who has spent a lifetime navigating complexity, I found myself humbled and inspired by his clarity and heart. This book will challenge the way you think—and that's a good thing ."

—**Mark Johnson**, ESG., CCEP

"Reading *Fool for Thought* on my birthday was one of the greatest gifts I've received. The essays are simple, powerful, and deeply personal—written in a way that invites reflection and speaks across age, culture, and background. It feels less like a book and more like a meaningful conversation over coffee. Anyone who reads it will be better for it."

—**Gerado Monroy**, executive leader and early reader

"This book is full of wind—the kind of force that makes trees grow strong. You'll see yourself in it, and come out stronger for it."

—**Kevin Hadawi**, Senior Vice President – Investments, Wells Fargo Advisors

"It felt like more than a book—it was an experience. You'll want to sit with these essays, reflect, highlight, and grow. Honest, deeply relatable, and quietly transformative."

—**Kristin Curtis**, educator and lifelong learner

"This isn't a book that tells you what to think—it reminds you how important it is to reflect. The humility and self-awareness on every page is rare, and needed."

—**Jared Gwin**, business strategist and early reader

"David's words gave voice to the thoughts many of us carry quietly. This book reminded me that living intentionally creates space for clarity, healing, and grace. "

—**Janette Wold**, writer and personal growth coach

"There's something grounded and quietly powerful in these pages. *Fool for Thought* doesn't just reflect a journey—it invites the reader into it. David's writing offers clarity and calm, leaving you both inspired and wanting more. It's not a how-to. It's a hand held out in honesty ."

—**Leslie Nance**, Holistic Cancer Coach & Founder of AnyStageCancer.com

"It challenged me in the best way—this isn't a book of answers; it's a book that sharpens your questions. *Fool for Thought* gave me language for thoughts I hadn't yet articulated. It's rare to find something that meets you where you are and still moves you forward."

—**Brian Wegner**, Co-Founder & CEO of Kala

"I loved the brevity—but I kept wanting more. The themes are sharp, relatable, and authentic. This book opens the door for readers to see themselves in new light."

—**Victor Cantu**, *early reader and leadership advisor*

"David Vega doesn't hand you a map—he hands you a mirror. *Fool for Thought* reads like a quiet conversation over coffee, inviting you to slow down and wrestle with what truly matters. In a world addicted to quick fixes, David's humility and honesty are electric. As someone who's written four bestsellers, I found myself challenged, comforted, and reminded of why I started writing in the first place ."

—**Farshad Asl**, #1 Amazon Bestselling Author, Leadership Expert, International Speaker

"This book is uniquely outstanding! I loved the style, the messages, the ease of the writing—everything. If this book, with the simplicity and purity of its messages, doesn't end up on the *New York Times* bestseller list, I'll be shocked."

—**Tim Wallace**, lifelong reader and business leader

"It made me laugh, it brought me to tears, and it made me better. This book isn't just powerful—it's timeless. I'll be rereading it often and sharing it with others. It meets people exactly where they are."

—**Gerald Hendrik**, executive, mentor, and early reader

"I couldn't put it down. Your words made me think deeply— not just about you, but about myself. It's humbling to read something so authentic, so well-timed, and so full of quiet strength."

—**Mark Johnson**, entrepreneur and creative strategist

"I started reading, and I couldn't stop. Each essay invites reflection—and leaves you better for it. David's writing doesn't preach. It prompts. It helped me see my own mindset more clearly."

—**Jenny Miller**, organizational consultant and leadership coach

Editorial services provided by Anna Krusinski (https://editsbyanna.wordpress.com/).

Cover design by Adam Hay Studio, UK

Dedication

For Lucinda Guerrero Vega. My mother. My earliest believer. The original source of audacity in my story.

People sometimes call me audacious—though rarely in such flattering terms. More often, it sounds like: "You're crazy," or "That kind of hope will be devoured by reality."

But here's the thing: I am audacious. And I learned it from my mom.

She died when I was just seventeen. The memories have faded over the decades, but the impression she left never has. She was fierce. Not flawless, not always gentle—but fiercely determined. Her boldness could be jarring to those who crossed her, but I never saw her as some polished, perfect idol. I saw her as someone who was unafraid to speak her mind. Someone who didn't wait for permission. Someone who didn't apologize for her ambition. Someone who demanded equal footing long before it was common to do so.

She didn't get to finish the job of raising me. But she never gave up hope that I would grow up. And I like to think I've become the man I am, in great part, because of her.

When I stepped into the world as a young man, I was ill-prepared. I had no plan, little formal education, and no marketable skills. There was no trust fund—just the grit of survival and a $200 monthly Social Security survivor benefit. I was one of seven kids. And yet … my mom left me something far more valuable than money.

She left me the audacity to dream.

Not through speeches. Not through praise. But through her presence. Through her actions. Through her quiet but relentless belief: "I believe in you ... and you should too."

She modeled boldness. She lived with grit. And she taught me the most important truths I carry with me today: If you don't ask, it probably won't happen. If you're told no, keep going. And if you want something meaningful—something better—you'd better be ready to fight for it.

We didn't use the word *audacity* in my house when I was growing up. But I knew what it meant.
I called it *courage*.

She wasn't here for my most transformative years. But I've never felt alone.
Her belief in me echoes still.

CONTENTS

Foreword

Over the course of my life—serving in uniform for more than four decades and later working with veterans and their families—I've come to believe that true leadership begins with character and humility. These are not qualities you pick up in a classroom. They are earned over time through hardship, service, and the willingness to listen and learn.

That's why *Fool for Thought* spoke to me.

This isn't a book filled with ego or empty motivation. It's a series of honest reflections by someone who's been in the trenches—professionally and personally—and has chosen to think deeply about what those experiences mean. David Vega writes from a place of lived experience, not theory. And he does so with a level of sincerity that's increasingly rare in today's fast-paced, filtered world.

I first got to know David through his support of veterans and military families—men and women whose lives were changed forever by service and sacrifice. What struck me then, and what comes through clearly in this book, is his ability to see people—not just their roles, ranks, or résumés. He listens. He reflects. And more importantly, he encourages others to do the same.

This book invites you to think—not to be told what to think, but to pause and consider what really matters. It's for anyone seeking clarity in a noisy world, courage in uncertain times, or simply a reminder that our lives are shaped not just by what happens to us but by how we choose to respond.

Fool for Thought is not about having all the answers. It's about asking better questions. And in that pursuit, I believe David offers something of real value—especially for those willing to slow down and reflect.

I'm honored to write this foreword. And I hope that as you turn these pages, you find something that stirs your own thinking, challenges your assumptions, or brings light to a part of your journey you hadn't fully considered.

Let the reflection begin.

— Lieutenant General Leroy Sisco, USA (Ret.)

Preface

This book began quietly.

Not with a grand ambition or an outlined thesis, but with the gentle push of mortality, a desire to leave something behind for my children, and a lifelong habit of turning questions over in my mind until they soften into insight. At first, these were just notes—fragments of ideas scribbled in journals, half-formed reflections sent as texts, or thoughts I couldn't shake after a conversation or a quiet morning drive.

What you now hold is a curated collection of those thoughts—some lived, others observed; some hard-earned, others still unsettled. I didn't set out to write a book for the world. I set out to write a few things down before I ran out of time. The fact that it evolved into something more speaks not to my mastery but to how universal certain questions really are.

This isn't a memoir, though pieces of my life appear throughout. It isn't a how-to, nor is it prescriptive. I don't want to tell you what to think. I only hope to offer a moment's pause—to help you consider your own thinking a little more deeply, and perhaps find some courage where doubt used to live.

If the writing here feels unfinished, good. That's intentional. I believe the best questions are the ones still unfolding—and the best conversations are the ones we're still having.

Introduction

Life doesn't wait until you're ready. It just shows up—with questions, with challenges, with change.

Last year, I fainted in my bathroom, cracked my head on the tile floor, and woke up in the ICU with a brain bleed. Not long after, I was diagnosed with prostate cancer. Thankfully, the prognosis is good, but those two wake-up calls arrived back-to-back as loud reminders that time is not promised.

That's when I felt the urge to write this book.

Fool for Thought wasn't born from expertise. It was born from urgency, from the desire to make sense of a life shaped by both pain and purpose. These essays are my attempt to explore the questions that have shaped me: What does it mean to lead without ego? To live with intention? To find meaning in moments that don't make sense?

I wrote this for anyone who's ever felt offtrack, overly pressured, or quietly overwhelmed. For people who've succeeded on paper but still feel like something's missing. For those who want to think more clearly, live more intentionally, and carry their story with a little more grace.

This isn't a guidebook. It's not a manifesto. It's a reflection. A conversation. A collection of honest essays on life, leadership, loss, and learning—anchored not in answers but in curiosity.

If you're looking for something prescriptive, you won't find it here. But you will find the following:

Vega – Fool for Thought

- Space to slow down and think deeply

- Language for what you've felt but haven't yet named

- A companion in the contradictions and questions that shape us

This book won't give you a blueprint. But it might help you see your own life a little more clearly—and walk forward with more grace.

I called it *Fool for Thought* because I don't claim to have it all figured out. In a world obsessed with certainty, I think there's value in staying open—in thinking out loud, in choosing humility, and in daring to reflect.

You may notice patterns in how I write—there's a rhythm to reflection that appeals to my analytical nature, and I've leaned into it. Not to make things predictable, but to help each insight land with clarity and intention.

Though I believe this book offers the most when it is read in full, it wasn't designed to be linear. Each section stands on its own. You can read the essays in order—or jump to a part that speaks to your current moment—and still find meaning, insight, or just a small space to breathe.

If these pages do anything, I hope they invite you to slow down, ask better questions, and reconnect with the quiet wisdom inside you.

Welcome to the conversation.

Part I: The Art of Thinking

Thinking is more than problem-solving—it's how we shape meaning, identity, and direction. These first essays explore the act of thinking itself: where it begins, why it matters, and how reflection can become a tool for personal growth. Before we build outward, we begin here—with the quiet discipline of thought.

Essay 1: What Is Thinking?

I was five years old, sitting in my kindergarten class at Henry B. Gonzales Elementary, when I decided I would marry a girl in my class. I didn't know what marriage meant, but my mind raced ahead anyway, dreaming up the house we'd live in, the adventures we'd have, and even the names of our kids. I remember staring out the window, lost in the story I was quietly building. I didn't realize it at the time, but I was practicing something I'd come to rely on my whole life: the act of thinking. The quiet, imaginative kind. The kind that makes sense of the world before you even know the words for it.

Thinking, for me, is like a river—sometimes it flows freely and with imagination; sometimes it is slowed by obstacles; yet it is always shaping the landscape of our lives. As a child, I discovered its power in daydreams like the one I described above. As an adult, I've learned to navigate its currents more deliberately by using it to analyze, decide, and find meaning in a complex world.

Don't we all start this way? As children, our thoughts flow freely, painting possibilities without fear of practicality. When did you last let your mind wander like that—dreaming without limits, just to see where it would go? That freedom is where thinking begins. A river of imagination that carries us toward who we might become.

Years later, I stumbled across Descartes's famous phrase: "I think, therefore I am." And something clicked. This wasn't just about intellectualism; it was about identity. If thinking confirmed my existence, then *how* I thought could shape who I became. That idea became an anchor for me, especially as the river of my mind grew deeper, more turbulent, and more strongly shaped by experience.

As I grew older, thinking became less about dreaming and more about decision-making. I've always been a deliberate thinker, the kind of person who loves a good spreadsheet. When I buy a car, I'll spend weeks comparing models, prices, and features, not just to get the best deal but to get it right. I weigh every possibility, mapping the decision like a river's course.

How do you make big choices? Do you chart every path, or do you trust the current to guide you?

But life doesn't always give us the luxury of deliberation. As a young professional, I was juggling meetings, deadlines, and decisions without time to think them all through. That's when I came across psychologist Daniel Kahneman's distinction between System 1 and System 2 thinking. One is fast and intuitive. The other is slow and analytical. It helped me make sense of how I moved between instinct and reason—how sometimes I was flowing freely with the current, and other times, I had to paddle upstream.

Even now, I notice it. In the chaos of the day, I make quick calls; System 1 in action. But in the quiet moments, I reflect and let System 2 do its work. The dance between the two is universal, isn't it? We all toggle between acting on gut and pausing to reflect, each mode shaping our path.
Distractions, though, can muddy the waters. A phone call. A stray worry. An interruption. They scatter your focus, pulling

you out of flow. Managing that is still a practice for me—one I haven't mastered yet.

Life's hardest moments test the river's strength.

My father left when I was young, abandoning me both emotionally and financially. His absence left a silent ache within me. Then, at seventeen, my mother died in a car accident. And for a long time, it felt like the river of my thoughts had dried up completely. I didn't know how to move forward. I was angry. Grieving. Stuck.

In my twenties and thirties, I coped the best I could through work, relationships, and grit. But there was an undercurrent I couldn't escape. Then, in my early forties—twenty-five years after my mother's death—I read Viktor Frankl's *Man's Search for Meaning*. A Holocaust survivor, Frankl wrote that, even in suffering, we can choose our response. That idea cracked something open in me. I couldn't undo the pain, but I could choose what it would mean.

I chose not to be a victim. I chose to live in a way that honored my mother's love.

Have you ever faced a moment like that? One where thinking helped you move through pain, not to erase it but to find meaning in it? Frankl reminded me that thinking isn't just about solving problems. It's about choosing who we become in the face of life's hardest questions.

So, what is thinking?

It's a river that flows through every part of life—imagination, decision, and resilience. It's not just an act. It's a *practice*—a way of engaging with the world. My thoughts have been my companions—sometimes clear, sometimes turbulent, always shaping my path. From childhood dreams to adult choices, from grief to growth, thinking has helped me make sense of it all.

As I write this, I'm embarking on a series of essays to explore thinking's many facets—how it shapes our relationships, fuels creativity, and guides us through uncertainty. I invite you to join me.

Reflect on your own river of thought.

How has it shaped your life?

What currents carry you forward, and what obstacles do you navigate?

Thinking isn't just a tool. It's a journey.

And it might just be the way we discover who we are—and who we can still become.

What do you think?

When was the last time you let your thoughts wander freely? What did you discover in the process?

Essay 2: Why I Write to Reflect

I don't write because I have all the answers.
I write because I have questions, and writing helps me sit
with them long enough to learn something true.

It started with lyrics.
I was young and was trying to emulate the way a clever line
in a song could spark a feeling or paint a picture. I didn't yet
have the words for what I was doing, but I knew when they
worked. And in time, those early stabs at songwriting became
something else: poetry. Mostly for loved ones. Sometimes
just for myself. Observations, tributes, and cryptic thoughts
about life that felt bigger than I could explain.

Even though I had an appreciation for poetry in a lyrical
sense, it wasn't until college that I discovered William Blake,
and everything changed.

I was struggling in a British literature class, especially with
interpretations that didn't resonate with me. So I buried
myself in the library and read every critical analysis I could
find of Blake's work, trying to piece the puzzle together. I'm
not sure I ever cracked the code, but when I finally shared
my perspective—a view apparently no one else had
offered—my professor held it in high praise. That moment
changed something fundamental in me.

It taught me that writing to reflect isn't about guessing the
right answer.
It is about being *honest enough* to offer your own.

Vega – Fool for Thought

For most of my life, I processed things silently. I carried thoughts in my head, sorted emotions in private, and tried to "figure it out" on the go. But over time, I started to notice something: Until I wrote something down, it stayed vague. A feeling. A hunch. A swirl of thought with no clear shape.

Writing gave it shape.
It slowed me down. It made me listen to myself. Not just the surface chatter but the deeper truths underneath—the ones I sometimes avoided or didn't know how to name.

I don't write to impress. I write to understand.
And I've found that when I'm honest on the page, I discover things I didn't even know I believed.

Reflection through writing has helped me make peace with the past, see patterns I couldn't name before, and ask better questions about the kind of man, leader, husband, and father I want to be. It's helped me grieve with clarity and celebrate with gratitude.

Sometimes it's a single line that unlocks something. Other times, it takes pages. But the act itself—putting thought into language—forces me to wrestle, refine, and ultimately grow.

It's become my mirror.
And in a world that moves quickly and speaks loudly, it's one of the few places where I can still hear myself think.

So I write to reflect.
To pause.
To return to myself—and hopefully, to offer something others can return to as well.

Because if there's one thing I've learned, it's this:
The more honest I am on the page, the more connected others
feel when they read it.
And that's a kind of reflection worth sharing.

What do you think?

*What insight or emotion have you only come to understand
after writing it down?*

Part II: Personal Growth and Self-Discovery

We're all works in progress. These essays are reflections on how I've grown through stumbles, self-doubt, and moments of clarity. They're not a blueprint but a mirror. What I've learned is this: Self-awareness isn't a destination. It's a daily decision to stay honest with yourself and be brave enough to evolve.

Essay 3: The Journey of Self-Awareness

It's a strange thing to spend your whole life with yourself and still be discovering who you are.

I used to think self-awareness was a trait. Something you either had or didn't. But now I see it as a journey. A process. A practice. One that doesn't end just because you've had a breakthrough or read the right book. In fact, the deeper I go, the more I realize how much more there is to uncover.

For a long time, I measured myself by what others reflected back to me. Receiving praise meant I was doing well. Receiving silence meant I wasn't enough. Criticism? That cut deep, and usually confirmed my own self-doubt. I let the outside world define my inside world.

But eventually, life forced a different kind of honesty. Through mistakes. Through conflict. Through unexpected success. I started noticing patterns in how I responded under stress, why certain conversations triggered me, and where I was seeking validation instead of connection.

It wasn't always flattering.
But it was freeing.

Self-awareness, I've found, begins with humility—the willingness to see yourself clearly, even when it's uncomfortable. It deepens with courage—the ability to keep looking even when what you find doesn't match who you thought you were. And it grows with grace—the understanding that knowing yourself isn't about perfection, it's about alignment.

One of the most influential ideas I've encountered on this journey comes from Adam Smith's *The Theory of Moral Sentiments*. He brilliantly posits that human morality arises from sympathy—our ability to imagine ourselves in others' situations. At the center of this view is the "impartial spectator," a kind of internal moral compass that helps us balance our self-interest with our concern for others. It's that voice inside us—not always loud, but always watching—that asks: *Would you judge someone else the same way you're justifying this to yourself?*

Smith's insight gave language to something I was beginning to experience: that self-awareness isn't just about understanding yourself. It's about holding yourself accountable through a lens that's both honest and fair. Not harsh. Not ego-driven. But principled.

It's not enough to *know* your strengths. You have to understand your blind spots. Your habits. The stories you tell yourself about who you are and what you deserve.

And maybe most importantly, you have to be willing to revise those stories as you grow.

The journey of self-awareness is less about arriving and more about returning to yourself, to your values, to the quiet truths that get buried beneath noise, ego, and fear. Every season reveals something new. Every failure holds a mirror. Every relationship teaches you something—if you're paying attention.

I'm still learning.
Still uncovering.
Still catching myself mid-pattern and choosing, sometimes awkwardly, a better response.

That, to me, is the work.
Not becoming someone new, but becoming more honest about who you already are.
And giving yourself permission to evolve.

Pause and reflect:

What's one pattern or reaction in your life that you've recently become more aware of?

Essay 4: Finding Purpose Without a Road Map

I didn't chart my course.
I didn't even finish high school.

At seventeen, I wasn't guided by ambition or clarity. I was guided by hunger, the humble kind that asks only for peace, for a steady job, and for the soft landing life never promised me. I wasn't chasing purpose. I was chasing a paycheck. A little dignity. A reason to believe things could get better. My future felt out of reach, buried beneath the weight of a past I couldn't stop revisiting.

There was no vision board. No master plan. Just motion.

And still … the path unfolded. Not as a golden road but as a trail scratched out with calloused hands and late nights. Purpose didn't call to me from the horizon. It whispered from behind: *Keep going. You'll understand later.*

After my mother died, I sank. Not in spectacle but in silence. I stopped hoping. Let go of the rope. Drifted.

What pulled me back wasn't thunder. It was the quiet resilience of people who had every reason to quit but didn't. Who showed me that sometimes survival isn't just about making it, it's about remaking yourself along the way.

I remember a neighbor, Rodney, who died in a car accident when we were both sixteen. We weren't close, we ran in

29

different circles—but there was a mutual respect between us, an unspoken sense that we each saw something worthwhile in the other. At his funeral, I watched his mother stand with a kind of strength I didn't fully understand at the time. She was hurting, clearly, but she was not broken. She held tightly to her faith, spoke kindly to everyone, and even found space to comfort others. A year later, when I lost my own mother, it was her presence I remembered. That kind of strength— quiet, faithful, and unwavering—showed me what it looked like to carry pain without being consumed by it.

I didn't leap into a better life. I stepped into it. Hesitantly. Repeatedly.

The jobs that felt like detours became teachers. The roles I thought I wasn't ready for became mirrors. Even the seasons of wandering held value, planting seeds that wouldn't bloom until much later.

And that's how purpose works, I think. It doesn't present itself with clarity, but with clues. It doesn't arrive—it accumulates. Like layers of sediment shaped by time, by pressure, and by choice.

We speak of "finding" purpose. But purpose isn't lost. It's *built*. In the questions we keep asking. In the courage to keep walking. In the willingness to become more than what the world expected of us.

I didn't have a road map.
But I walked anyway.
And looking back, that's what purpose really is.

Vega – Fool for Thought

Not a place but a direction.
Not a calling but a quiet decision to answer—again and again.

Not something you wait to receive.
But something you *create*. Every step, every stumble, and every time you begin again.

Pause and reflect:

Can you identify a moment that didn't feel important at the time—but shaped your direction?

Essay 5: Redefining Success

For a long time, success was a scoreboard.
A salary. A title. A list of milestones that could be rattled off in polite conversation.

I chased those things—not because I was shallow but because I thought that's what you were supposed to do. Achieve. Accumulate. Prove yourself. Then, eventually, you'd feel it: *success.*

After earning my college degree, an entirely new world opened up to me. It was both inspiring and a little depressing. On the one hand, my new career trajectory was placing me in a position to earn a level of wealth my parents could have only dreamed of. It was as if a life I had once viewed as real—but not meant for *our kind*—was suddenly within reach.

But that double-edged sword changed me in ways I hadn't anticipated.

As I climbed the ladder, I began to learn how much my superiors were making—and in some cases, my peers. I started to measure my worth almost exclusively in dollars. I wouldn't have admitted it then, but the number on my paycheck became the shorthand for my success. It was addictive, rewarding, and yet … hollow.

Because as I rose, something else started happening.

I began to see that the work I was doing wasn't just changing my life, it was positively impacting the lives of others. The financial security I had once craved became less motivating than the human ripple I was creating.

I don't recall the exact moment when the shift happened. Maybe it happened over years. But at some point, I found myself devoting less energy to chasing the next raise, and more energy to considering my contribution—what I was building and *who* I was helping along the way. That shift changed me in ways I never could have imagined.

So when I finally hit some of those early milestones, something unexpected happened. The satisfaction was there, but it didn't last. It faded more quickly than I'd expected. And I was left with a quiet, uncomfortable question: *Is this all it is?*

That question became a turning point.

It made me look beyond the scoreboard. Beyond how things looked from the outside. It pushed me to redefine what success meant—not in general but for *me*. And the more I reflected, the more I realized: The most meaningful moments in my life weren't the ones that boosted my résumé. They were the ones that expanded my soul.

A tough but honest conversation with someone I loved.
A project that aligned with my values—even if it didn't pay the most.
The decision to prioritize my family over optics.
The growth that came from failure, not from applause.

I've come to believe that real success isn't a destination. It's a direction. A sense of alignment between your values, your work, and your relationships. It's knowing who you are and showing up that way—even when no one's watching.

By that measure, some of the wealthiest people I've known were empty.
And some of the "ordinary" people I've met were quietly extraordinary.

Success, I've learned, is personal.
You define it. You build it. And you refine it as you go.

For me, it's now less about what I've accomplished and more about who I'm becoming.
It's about living in a way that feels true, not just impressive.
And making sure that when I lay my head down at night, I like the man I'm becoming.

That's the kind of success no title can give—and no failure can take away.

Pause and reflect:

How has your personal definition of success changed in the past five years?

Essay 6: The Power of Small Decisions

Most people think life is shaped by the big moments—
graduations, job offers, weddings, or crises.
And while those moments matter, I've come to believe that
life is actually built in the in-between.

Not the headline events but the footnotes.
Not the big leaps but the small steps.

The decision to show up when it would've been easier to stay
home.
The moment when you bite your tongue instead of lashing
out.
The phone call you return. The late-night book you read.
The apology you offer—even if it's not fully your fault.

These choices rarely feel important in the moment. But when
strung together over time, they become the story of who you
are.

One of the most vivid reminders of this came to me during a
charity auction, of all places. My wife and I were attending a
local nonprofit fundraiser—a night of giving, laughter, and
raffle tickets. I raised my hand to bid on a trip to Cross
Timbers, Missouri: one thousand acres with a working cattle
ranch, private chef, ATVs, fishing, and starry skies. A place
so remote that my wife asked, "Why would we go there?"

I didn't have a great answer. Just a gut feeling that this could
be something different.

We won the trip.

That simple decision—to make a half-playful bid at a charity event—led to one of the most meaningful experiences of our lives. Not because of the landscape (though it was stunning) but because of the people we brought with us. Friends. Family. Coworkers. Different corners of our life converged in one place.

Every morning brought stillness. Every night brought connection.
The conversations. The firelight. The laughter of kids exploring a world beyond screens.

I remember sitting on the back porch, with the morning sun spilling over the pasture, and experiencing a silence so absolute that it felt like the world was holding its breath. That's when it hit me: I had never heard my own thoughts that clearly before.

It reminded me that sometimes joy isn't found in exotic destinations, it's found in unexpected detours.

That trip didn't just give us a memory. It reminded us how we want to live.

Small decision. Big impact.

And sometimes those small decisions don't just lead to connection, they lead to survival.

There have been days in my life when darkness has pressed hard. When I've felt alone. When getting out of bed required everything I had. In those moments, what saved me wasn't a grand breakthrough, it was a single, quiet choice: *Don't give up.*

Vega – Fool for Thought

There's a poem I turn to when things feel especially heavy.
"Invictus" by William Ernest Henley.
One line always stops me:

My head is bloody, but unbowed.

It's a reminder that while I can't always control what
happens to me, I can always control my next move. And
sometimes that next move is just … standing back up.

Some of the biggest changes in my life started with small
decisions. A conversation I almost skipped. A job I nearly
turned down. A book I picked up on impulse. None of them
felt life-altering at the time. But they were. Looking back, I
can draw a direct line from those tiny turning points to major
chapters in my journey.

It's humbling—and a little unsettling—to realize that your
future might hang on something that doesn't feel significant.
But it's also empowering.

Because it means you're never really stuck waiting for a
perfect moment to act.
You're always one small choice away from a new direction.

The challenge is that small decisions don't usually come with
fanfare.
They require you to believe in the long game.
To trust that choosing well in the moment—however
ordinary—can lead to something extraordinary down the line.

You don't need to predict the future.
You just need to move with intention.

So if you're facing something that seems small, pay attention.
Small doesn't mean unimportant.
It means foundational.

And often, it's in those quiet choices that our loudest victories are born.

Pause and reflect:

What small decision in your past ended up having a big impact on your life?

Part III: Leadership and Influence

Leadership isn't about titles or charisma—it's about presence. The kind that builds trust, steadies the room, and lifts others even when no one's watching. These essays explore what it means to lead from character, not ego—and how influence often comes from consistency, not from volume.

Essay 7: Leading Without Authority

Early in my career, I was under the delusion that a title would equate to power.

And in fairness, that's what I saw around me. Hierarchy mattered. The people with bigger offices made bigger decisions. It seemed obvious: If you wanted to lead, you had to climb.

So I chased the title.

And when I got my first management role, I thought I was set.

Then I climbed a little higher—and thought it would get easier. After all, it was about the role now, not the man. Right?

Wrong.

What I began to realize—painfully at times—is that leadership isn't measured by your place on the organizational chart. It's measured by your ability to influence positive outcomes. It's not about control. It's about presence.

As I advanced, I started observing the people who led *well*—the ones others naturally gravitated toward, regardless of their position. The people who didn't need to raise their voices or flash their titles. They didn't force things—they shaped them. Their influence came from who they were, not what they were called.

And I'll admit: I didn't always get it right.

I had moments when I drifted from servant leader to servant *master*—when the title got to my head, or I thought I had to assert dominance to be effective. Thankfully, I had mentors who called me out. They were brutally honest, in the best way. And because of them, I started to change.

Some of the best leaders I've ever known didn't have titles. They didn't run meetings, sign checks, or sit at the head of the table. But they had something you could feel the moment they entered a room: *influence.*

What sets great leaders apart isn't power, it's the presence they bring to every moment.

And authority isn't something you're given. It's something you *earn*—one interaction at a time.

I used to think leadership was something you stepped into once you had the title. So I waited. I deferred. I kept my head down, thinking my chance would come later—once I got the promotion or the official nod.

But what I didn't realize was that leadership opportunities were everywhere. They just didn't look the way I expected them to.

I started to see them in the following ways:

- In the way you treat someone who can't offer you anything in return

- In the calm you bring to a tense moment

- In having the courage to speak up when everyone else is staying quiet

- In lifting someone up without needing credit

You don't need authority to lead.
You need clarity about who you are and what you stand for.

Once I began showing up with that mindset, things changed.
Not overnight. Not dramatically. But consistently. People
started listening more. Trusting more. Asking more. And
eventually, yes, opportunities came, but not because I chased
them. Because I practiced leadership before I had the title.

Leadership without authority is often the most powerful kind.
Because it's not dependent on structure.
It's not fueled by fear.
It's grounded in character.

It's easy to lead when people *have* to follow you.
But when people *choose* to follow you—even without
obligation, that's when you know you're leading well.

So wherever you are, whatever role you're in—remember:
You don't have to wait for permission to lead.
You just have to choose how you show up.
The rest tends to follow.

Your turn:

*How have you led or influenced others even without holding
a formal title?*

Essay 8: The Quiet Leader

Not all leaders are loud.
Some don't command the room; they steady it.
They don't speak first—they listen longer.
They don't chase attention, but when they do speak, people lean in.

For a long time, I thought leadership had to be loud. Assertive. Out front. That's what we're shown—the bold visionary, the charismatic speaker, the one who dominates space. And while there's value in that, I've learned it's not the only way. In fact, it's not even the most effective way for everyone.

Hello, my name is David, and I'm a recovering introvert.

I say that with a wink, but I mean it. Society tends to praise extroverts, the talkers, the networkers, and the natural charmers. And don't get me wrong, I like them too. After all, they do most of the talking … and I'm a great listener.

But if you know me well, you know I'm shy—not timid, but inward by nature. Like any human, I enjoy social connection. I just don't need as much of it, and it takes energy to show up in loud rooms with big personalities. When I tell people I'm an introvert, the usual response is a chuckle. "Really?" And I walk away, wondering if I convinced them or not.

Early in my career, I saw my quiet nature as a disadvantage. I worried people would mistake it for passivity—or worse, weakness. I didn't want to be overlooked. But I also didn't want to pretend to be someone I wasn't.

Over time, though, I began to notice something.

The quiet leader doesn't seek control; they build trust.
They don't need the spotlight; they give it away.
They create space instead of filling it—and in that space, people rise.

What I've found is that quiet leadership isn't about volume—it's about consistency. It's about having the strength to hold your values under pressure. The willingness to support others without the need for credit. The patience to listen fully before responding. And the courage to lead from conviction, not from ego.

I've learned how to adapt, too. When I walk into a crowded room, I instinctively scan for energy. I seek out the talkers, because once they get going, they make the conversation easy. And I always try to find the quiet ones, too—the other introverts in the corner—because I know what it feels like to be overlooked. I'll be the extrovert for them.

Some of the most influential people in my life didn't talk the most—they listened best. They led by example. By steadiness. By integrity. And they made me feel seen.

I've tried to lead in the same way.

Over time, I've learned that being an introvert doesn't mean being invisible. It just means I recharge differently. While an extrovert walks out of a party feeling lit up, I often walk out needing silence. But here's the twist: Introverts can thrive socially. We can lead. We can host. We can command attention. It just takes a little more intention—and a little more recovery time afterward.

Being a quiet leader doesn't mean you lack impact. It means your impact is often felt, not announced. And while the noise might get more attention in the moment, it's the quiet presence that tends to last.

So if your voice isn't the loudest in the room, don't count yourself out.
Leadership isn't about volume.
It's about vision, values, and how you carry both, especially when no one's watching.

Your turn:

When has quiet leadership—your own or someone else's—made a meaningful difference?

Essay 9: The Importance of Mentorship

Nobody makes it alone. Not really.

For every success story, there's often someone in the background—quietly opening a door, offering a hand, or asking the right question at the right time.

That's the power of mentorship.

I've had mentors who didn't even know they were mentoring me. Some taught me through a single conversation. Others, through years of steady presence. But each one left a mark. They helped me see possibilities I hadn't considered. They challenged my assumptions. And, maybe most importantly, they believed in me at times when I wasn't sure I should believe in myself.

That kind of belief is powerful.

Because sometimes all it takes is for one person to say, "You've got something."
And suddenly, you start to believe it too.

I think about Dr. Gary Raffaele, who helped shape my worldview back in college—not just through coursework, but through real exposure to nonprofit leadership and the ethics of giving back. Or Frank Valtierra, my older brother, who stepped in during the darkest stretch of my youth—not as a mentor by title but through sacrifice and love.

I remember Johnny Gabriel, a small business owner who gave me both a job and an unexpected financial gift to keep

46

me in college. And people like Ken Eakes, who steadied me backstage before one of the most meaningful speeches of my life—not with advice but with a quiet prayer that gave me peace.

There are dozens of others—some executives who shaped my leadership philosophy, and some friends who simply showed up at the right time and stayed long enough for me to rise.

Mentorship isn't always formal. It doesn't require a program or a contract. At its core, it's a relationship built on trust, honesty, and a shared commitment to growth. A good mentor doesn't just give answers. They ask better questions. They don't try to shape you into a copy of themselves—they help you become more of who you already are.

I've been fortunate to have mentors across different seasons of my life—some in business, some in faith, and some in personal resilience. Each one brought a different lens, but the impact was the same: They saw me, challenged me, and walked with me just far enough to help me move forward.

Now I try to do the same for others.

Because if I've learned anything, it's this: Mentorship isn't just something you receive. It's something you eventually owe. Not out of obligation but out of gratitude. Out of recognition that someone once saw potential in you—and now it's your turn to pass that forward.

The ripple effect of mentorship can't always be measured. But it can be felt.
Sometimes for a lifetime.

Your turn:

Who has believed in you when you didn't believe in yourself, and how did it shape your path?

Part IV: Identity, Beliefs, and Open-Mindedness

Identity isn't fixed—it's layered, it evolves, and it's sometimes messy. In these essays, I wrestle with culture, belief, and the discomfort of difference. What I've found is this: Understanding others often starts with understanding yourself. And open-mindedness doesn't mean losing your footing—it means being willing to grow.

Essay 10: Honoring My Heritage Without Losing Myself

I'm proud of where I come from.
But I've also wrestled with it.

When I was growing up, my identity was shaped by both what I was and by what others assumed I was. My name, my skin color, and my background—they all carried stories before I even had the chance to tell my own.

Sometimes that meant being underestimated.
Sometimes it meant being tokenized.
Sometimes it meant being expected to speak for an entire group when all I really wanted was to speak for myself.

I used to feel like I had to pick a lane: fully lean into my heritage, or set it aside to "fit in." I didn't always see space for nuance. But as I got older, I began to understand that identity doesn't have to be an either/or. It can be a both/and.

I can honor my roots without being boxed in by them.
I can carry the culture that raised me and still grow into something more.
I can be proud of my background, and still believe that it doesn't determine my ceiling.

That's the balance I've learned to walk.
Not to minimize where I come from but to stop letting others define what that means for me. My heritage informs my story, but it doesn't write all of it.

Vega – Fool for Thought

Recently, while reading *The Spanish Conquerors* by Irving Berdine Richman, I started thinking about the story buried in my DNA. My roots stretch back to Spain—places like Andalusia, Galicia, and Castile. My ancestors likely crossed the Atlantic in the 1500s. Were they settlers? Soldiers? Missionaries? I don't know. But they came—swept into the tide of conquest, migration, and history.

They didn't arrive in an empty land.
They encountered the Indigenous peoples of Mexico—rich in culture, wisdom, and ancient tradition. From that convergence—often uneasy, often unjust—a new identity emerged: *mestizo.*

I carry that legacy.

At six feet two inches tall, with curly black hair and what some would describe as "exotic" features, I've never quite matched the stereotypical image many Texans associate with Mexican heritage. My presence—my very face—is a reminder of convergence. Of blending and bending throughout history.

I am American by birth. Texan by pride. Mexican by legacy. Spanish by the passage of time.
These are not contradictions. They are layers.

And I've come to believe that identity—true identity—is never singular.
It's not fixed. It's evolving.

There's strength in remembering.
And freedom in evolving.

Vega – Fool for Thought

I want to carry my heritage with dignity—not as a chip on my shoulder but as a quiet reminder of resilience, grit, and generational hope. I want to show others—especially younger versions of me—that you don't have to choose between who you are and who you're becoming.

You can be both.

And in doing so, you don't erase your identity—you expand it.

Because your story isn't just where you live. It's who you come from.
It's what you carry.
And for me, it's what I choose to honor.

Consider this:

In what ways has your heritage shaped who you are today, and how do you carry it forward?

Essay 11: The Strength in Feeling Different

I used to sit on the floor just outside the bathroom door while my mom got ready for work. Her scent—Aqua Net, cinnamon, and instant coffee—filled the hallway before she ever said a word. I didn't know it then, but I was memorizing her strength. She never talked about sacrifice. She didn't need to. It was woven into her mornings, her movements, her quiet consistency. Before I ever knew what resilience meant, I had already seen it.

For most of my life, I've known what it feels like to be the "only one."
The only person of color in a meeting.
The only quiet voice in a room full of extroverts.
The only person with a different story, a different rhythm, or a different lens.

At first, I saw it as a liability.
Being different meant being exposed. It meant more eyes, more assumptions, and more pressure to prove I belonged. I used to wonder: Wouldn't it be easier to blend in? To talk like they talk, think like they think, and dress like they dress?

And I tried for a while.

But the more I did, the more I lost sight of myself.

What I've come to realize is that my difference didn't just come from how I looked or how I spoke—it came from how I was raised, and what I had to unlearn along the way.

53

Vega – Fool for Thought

My mother died when I was young, but her presence never left. She was fierce, unapologetically bold, and audacious in the way she navigated life. She didn't wait for permission. She didn't soften her ambition. And even though I had so little by way of formal preparation—no trust fund, limited education, just a survivor's benefit and a few hard-won lessons—I inherited something more valuable than security.

I inherited courage.

That early inheritance gave me the audacity to dream. To walk into rooms I wasn't "supposed" to belong in. To keep showing up, even when I was dismissed, doubted, or disregarded.

But I didn't always handle it well.

For a stretch in my life, I clung to certainty like it was a life raft. I needed to be right—about everything. Being wrong didn't just feel incorrect; it felt like failure. And failure, to someone who had grown up without safety, felt intolerable. So I controlled what I could—my image, my arguments, and my emotional armor.

Eventually, I learned that that kind of control is an illusion. And worse—it cuts you off from the very connection that makes life meaningful. I learned through failure, through conversations that could have brought me closer but didn't, and through pride that got in the way of progress. Slowly, I came to understand that humility is not weakness—it's strength. And difference is not something to conceal—it's something to carry with honor.

Vega – Fool for Thought

Feeling different can be lonely.
But over time, I started to realize it could also be a kind of superpower.

It gave me perspective.
It helped me see things others had missed.
It made me adaptable—able to navigate different rooms, speak different languages (figuratively and literally), and connect across divides.

It made me empathetic, too.
Because once you've been the one on the outside, you never forget how that feels—and you tend to look out for others who feel the same.

The truth is, we spend so much time trying to belong that we forget to ask what we're trying to belong to—and whether it's even worth it.

The more I've embraced what makes me different, the more confident I've become in what I have to offer. Not in spite of my story—but because of it.

Being different doesn't mean being less.
It doesn't mean being wrong.
It means having perspective. Depth. Uniqueness.
And sometimes it means having strength that has been forged in places others haven't had to walk through.

I've come to see difference not as something to explain away—but as a kind of quiet light.
It shines through the cracks, not around them.

So if you feel different—don't rush to fix it.
Sit with it.
Let it show you something others can't see.

Consider this:

When have you felt like the 'only one' in a room? How did you respond to that feeling?

Essay 12: Anchored Faith, Open Mind

I didn't grow up trying to save people.
I grew up trying to survive.

And somewhere in that struggle—amid the setbacks, the silences, and the occasional spark of hope—I found faith.

Not the kind that shouts from street corners or argues theology in comment sections. Mine was quieter. More personal. Less about proving and more about anchoring.

Faith, for me, has never been about having all the answers. It's been about having something to hold on to when the answers run out. Something to return to when the world stops making sense. Hearing a whisper when everything else is noise.

It came slowly—like a soup left to simmer.
I was baptized in the Catholic Church as a baby, just months after I was born. My family followed the traditions: catechism, first communion, and the appointment of my godfather. I didn't feel transformed, but my parents were proud.

Then came the unraveling.
A move to the country. My parents' divorce. A slow drift away from the Church, and eventually, from certainty. My father remarried and became emotionally distant. When my mother died in a tragic accident, I was seventeen. Alone. Just a two-hundred-dollar monthly survivor's benefit and a handful of couches to sleep on.

Vega – Fool for Thought

I wasn't searching for God—I was searching for peace. And faith seemed like my best chance at finding it.

The family who initially took me in were Pentecostal— warm, spirited, and generous with their hospitality and their hope. Their church was filled with music, energy, and invitation. It was healing in a way I didn't expect. But I still felt like a guest in someone else's tradition. I couldn't stay.

Over the years, I wandered. I explored Christianity in many forms. I studied Buddhism and touched the wisdom of Judaism, Islam, and Hinduism. I questioned Catholicism—its rituals, its wealth, and its treatment of women—but it remained the thread I returned to. Sometimes frayed. Sometimes tangled. But still tethered.

My mind and spirit don't always agree. I think deeply. I question everything. Logic often pulls one way while faith pulls the other way. But now and then, there are moments— quiet, unmistakable ones—when something stirs. A presence. A nudge. Something that feels like grace.

That's the thing about faith—it's not always a conviction. Sometimes it's a comfort.

Like tortilla soup, my faith isn't fancy. It's not perfect. It's made from scraps and seasons, stirred by grief, layered with questions, and slowly flavored by moments of meaning. Some ingredients came early. Others came late. But together, they've created something warm. Nourishing. Mine.

Still, here's what I know: The moment faith becomes a competition, it loses something essential. The need to convince someone else that my truth must become theirs

feels counter to everything my faith has taught me—
especially the part about love.

I've seen what happens when belief becomes a weapon.
When people preach without listening. When certainty leaves
no room for kindness. I want no part of that.

My faith gives me strength. It informs how I lead, how I
love, and how I forgive—especially when it's hard. But it's
not a blueprint I expect others to follow. I'd rather someone
feel safe in my presence than persuaded. I'd rather they leave
a conversation feeling seen, not cornered.

That doesn't mean I hide my faith. I just don't lead with a
sermon. I lead, hopefully, with how I live.

Sometimes people ask me about it. Sometimes they don't.
Either way, the goal isn't conversion—it's connection. And if
my faith means anything at all, it should show up in how I
treat others. Not just those who believe what I do—but
especially those who don't.

I believe in God.
I believe in grace.
And I believe that, like a good soup, real faith doesn't need to
be flashy. It just needs to be real—something that nourishes,
invites, and gives you strength to keep going.

Consider this:

*How do you balance being true to your faith with staying
open to new perspectives?*

Essay 13: Faith in the Face of Loss

There are questions I'll never be able to answer.
Why do some people suffer more than others?
Why is timing sometimes so cruel?
Why doesn't love always last?

Why don't good people always get what they deserve?

I've spent years trying to make sense of those questions. At first, I thought if I just read enough, worked hard enough, and did the right things, I'd find the answers. But the more life I live, the more I realize that meaning doesn't always come through understanding.

Sometimes it comes through faith.

Not blind faith. Not performative faith. But the kind that's been tested and still shows up. The kind that admits its doubts but keeps believing anyway.

I learned that lesson early.

As a kid, I thought time was endless. Summers stretched on forever, and the future felt infinite. The idea that anything— much less *everything*—was temporary felt unimaginable.

But impermanence introduced itself early in my life. My grandfather died when I was six. Two cousins died as teenagers. Those losses stung, but the real unraveling came when I was between sixteen and seventeen, when three people close to me died in separate car accidents.

The second loss shattered my world. The police knocked on our door. My mother had been killed in a crash. The woman who had carried me, protected me, and believed in me— gone, without warning.

I broke. Then I buried it. I had siblings to consider and responsibilities to shoulder as I was approaching adulthood in a world that kept moving while mine was standing still.

A neighbor's family took me in. They gave me support, structure, and hope. But tragedy struck again when their son, Troy, died in a freak go-kart accident. I left—not out of anger but because I couldn't bring more sorrow to a family that was already drowning in it.

Those years hollowed me out. I was angry. Adrift. Alone. And yet, something deeper stirred beneath the grief— something that kept me going even when I didn't understand *why*.

Faith.

Not the Sunday-school kind. The kind you hold on to because it's the only thing you've got left. A belief— sometimes fragile, sometimes fierce—that there's something more than chaos. That life isn't just random cruelty. That love doesn't vanish in the aftermath of loss.

Faith, for me, isn't about knowing everything.
It's about trusting that there's something greater at work, even when I can't see it.
It's about believing that love matters. That grace is real. That we're not alone in this world—even when we feel like we are.

Vega – Fool for Thought

Meaning didn't come all at once. It came in pieces. Through loss. Through rebuilding. Through moments when I was shown kindness I hadn't asked for and strength I hadn't thought I had. And slowly, I came to understand something that's anchored me ever since:

It's not about what you lose.
It's about what you *do* with the loss.
It's about what you gain in the aftermath.

Loss taught me to value presence.
Pain taught me to listen.
Faith taught me to stay open—even when life gave me every reason to shut down.

I've found that meaning rarely announces itself in a flash. It reveals itself in layers—through hardship, through service, and through quiet acts of kindness that ripple farther than we know. And often, faith is what gives those acts their weight. It's what connects the dots when life feels scattered. It's what steadies the ground when reason alone falls short.

I don't claim to know the full picture. But I've seen enough to believe there *is* a picture. That even in the chaos, something sacred is unfolding. And my job isn't to control it—it's to participate in it. To live with open hands. To love well. To stay grounded in something deeper than circumstance.

Faith doesn't remove pain.
But it gives pain a place to go.
It gives it shape, direction, and sometimes even purpose.

And in that space, meaning begins to emerge.

Consider this:

How has loss reshaped what you believe about life, love, or purpose?

Part V: Decision-Making and Problem Solving

We don't always get clarity before we act. More often, we move forward through the fog—guided by instinct as we traverse trials and a few stumbles along the way. These reflections are about risk, resilience, and the kind of wisdom you earn by living through uncertainty instead of avoiding it.

Essay 14: Learning to Embrace Uncertainty

There was a time in my life when I thought certainty was the goal.
If I could just get clear enough, plan well enough, and work hard enough—I'd finally reach the point where everything made sense. No more doubt. No more second-guessing. Just a straight path forward.

But life had other plans.

I've lived long enough to see that clarity often comes after the choice, not before it. And sometimes it never comes—or not in the way we hope. Some of the most meaningful decisions I've made began in complete uncertainty. I didn't know if I was ready. I didn't know if it would work. But I moved anyway.

That's the paradox of growth: It rarely waits for confidence. It demands courage in its absence.

I think about the first time I ever took a high-risk leap in my career when I joined a start-up backed by nothing more than a dream and some early stock options. It didn't come with a guarantee. Just long hours, lean pay, and the ever-present whisper: *What if this doesn't work?*

It wasn't easy. It wasn't even glamorous. But the decision to step into the unknown ended up unlocking not just financial reward—it also unlocked belief. Confidence. Momentum. And it left me with a gold watch—not as a flex but as a trophy of risk turned into growth. Here's a reminder: Belief, like compound interest, starts with small investments in courage.

But I didn't always have that courage. In fact, I began adulthood carrying the weight of loss and failure that was so heavy that uncertainty didn't feel optional—it felt like punishment.

I was broke, alone, and angry. I made reckless decisions, the kind that easily could have ended in tragedy. I wrecked my brother's car while driving drunk. I should've been done then. But slowly—through the grace of others and a stubborn refusal to give up—I started to rebuild.

Not because I had a plan. But because I chose to move forward anyway.

That's the thing about uncertainty—it doesn't just show up in the boardroom or at life's crossroad moments. It creeps in during healing. During reinvention. During moments when your hands are empty but your heart still beats with something hopeful.

Even recently, after a sudden fall and brain bleed landed me in the ICU, I was reminded again that nothing is certain. One moment, I was fine. The next, I was facing scans, surgeons, and fears I had never prepared for.

My recovery has been slow. Humbling. Quiet. But it has also been clarifying. Because sometimes uncertainty doesn't ask for your permission—it just shows up and asks who you'll become in its presence.

Uncertainty used to feel like failure. Like I was missing something everyone else had figured out. But over time, I started seeing it differently—not as a gap to close but as a space to explore.

Uncertainty, I've found, is where curiosity lives.
It's where innovation starts.
It's where humility becomes strength instead of weakness.

Think about it—every breakthrough, every reinvention, and every pivot that's changed the course of a life or a business or a relationship has started with the same basic truth:

We didn't know what would happen. And we did it anyway.

That doesn't mean abandoning reason or leaping blindly. It means holding space for not knowing, while still being willing to act. It means trusting that forward motion, even without a perfect plan, is better than standing still in fear.

I've come to see uncertainty not as the enemy of progress but as its companion.
It walks beside every worthwhile risk. Every new beginning. Every courageous step.

If you wait for certainty, you may never move.
If you embrace uncertainty, you may just discover something you couldn't see from where you started.

What do you think?

When was the last time you acted despite uncertainty, and what came of it?

Essay 15: When to Fight, When to Let Go

Some lessons in life are loud. Others sneak up on you.

This one came slowly, through experience: Not every battle is worth fighting. And not every loss is worth grieving.

For a long time, I thought persistence was always the answer. That having real strength meant holding on—pushing through, standing your ground, and proving your point. And to be fair, there are moments when that's true. There are things worth fighting for: your values, your family, and your dignity.

But over time, I learned that not all fights serve you. Some just drain you.

Letting go doesn't always mean giving up.
Sometimes it means choosing peace over pride.
Sometimes it means making room for something better.
Sometimes it means freeing yourself from something that was never yours to carry in the first place.

Years ago, I worked for a start-up that became an overwhelming success. Financially, yes—but more importantly, it gave me confidence. It validated the belief that I could take bold chances and win. That experience opened doors I never knew existed.

After we sold the company, I stayed on. The organization felt like family, and I imagined I'd be there indefinitely. Then, the new ownership arrived. And everything changed.

They offered me a lower role with less influence and a forced relocation to another state. I was still weighing it when the CEO flew in from headquarters and let me go. In person. It was framed kindly—almost like a favor. He told me I'd outgrown the company and that I was too big for the next chapter. And if I'm being honest, I didn't take it well. I smiled. I nodded. I played the good corporate citizen. But I cursed him under my breath.

Still, I took the severance. I accepted the story we agreed to tell—that I had chosen to move on. And as much as it stung at the time … he was right.

What felt like a shove turned out to be a springboard.

That exit cleared the way for one of the most transformative opportunities of my life. I don't know if he pushed me out for *his* good or *mine*, but it worked out beautifully for both of us. And because I chose to let go instead of fight back, I left with peace, not bitterness. That mindset gave me the freedom to step fully into what came next.

I've stayed in conversations too long, trying to win people over who were committed to misunderstanding me. I've clung to opportunities that looked good on paper but chipped away at my peace. I've tried to fix things that didn't want to be fixed. And each time, I learned the same thing:

Fighting harder doesn't always mean you're winning. Sometimes it just means you're stuck.

So how do you know the difference?

I've learned to ask a few questions:

Vega – Fool for Thought

- Am I fighting for something that matters, or just something I'm afraid to lose?

- Is this battle aligned with who I want to be, or just who I've been?

- If I let this go, will I feel less, or will I finally feel free?

The answers don't come easily. But they do come—with time, reflection, and honesty.

Some fights shape us.
Others wear us down.
The wisdom is knowing which is which.

And sometimes the bravest thing you'll ever do … is walk away still whole.

What do you think?

What are you holding on to that may be time to release—for your peace, not your pride?

Essay 16: Politics and Personal Identity: Can They Coexist?

I've lost count of how many times someone has assumed my politics—because of my skin color, my name, or a sliver of a sentence that was taken out of context. I've been labeled without speaking, sorted without a conversation, and quietly told—through a look or a joke—what "side" I must be on. And more than once, I've said nothing. Not because I lacked conviction but because I wasn't sure if nuance would survive the moment.

That's the cost of polarization: It teaches us to protect ourselves with silence.

I used to think politics was just about policy—tax rates, laws, and the economy.

Something abstract. Something far away. But I've lived long enough to see that politics isn't just about what happens in Washington. It's about what happens at kitchen tables, in classrooms, and in quiet decisions that shape who gets a chance—and who gets left behind.

Still, I hesitate to talk about politics.
Not because I don't have opinions—I do—but because I've seen how quickly the conversation can shift from talking about ideas to talking about identity. From "I disagree with your point" to "You must be one of them."

It's exhausting.
And dangerous.

Vega – Fool for Thought

When we tie our entire identity to a political label, something happens.
We stop thinking critically.
We defend the indefensible.
We start seeing "the other side" not as neighbors, colleagues, or fellow citizens but as enemies.

And maybe it's not just politics where this happens.
Maybe it's the same mechanism that leads us to confuse *belonging* with *being bound*.
Take sports: I'm a Dallas Cowboys fan. By all tribal logic, that should mean I "hate" the Philadelphia Eagles. And sure, I've got a few well-timed jokes ready for game day. But some of my dearest friends are Eagles fans—and a few are even from Philly. Our football allegiances are slices of our story. And sure, they're a part of who we are, but they don't define the whole pie.

The problem is, in politics, we forget that.
We treat every disagreement like an existential threat.
As if accepting a new cultural norm or policy idea somehow erases who we are.
As if compromise equals betrayal.

But I don't buy that.

Depending on the room, I've been called too conservative or too progressive. Too idealistic or too pragmatic. And honestly, I've taken those assertions as compliments.
Because the moment my views start fitting neatly into a box, I get suspicious. Not of others but of myself.

No one is one-dimensional.

I can care about fiscal responsibility and still believe in social safety nets.
I can support law enforcement and still demand accountability.
I can love my country and still want it to do better.

That tension? That's where real thinking happens.

I don't want to live in a world where every opinion is a litmus test.
I want to live in a world where people can wrestle with complexity without being labeled or dismissed. Where someone can say, "I see it differently," and still be invited to the table.

My identity is shaped by more than politics.
It's shaped by my faith, my culture, my family, and my lived experience.
And I try—however imperfectly—to offer that same grace to others.

Because in the end, the question isn't whether politics and personal identity can coexist.
They already do.

The real question is: Can *we* coexist, even when our identities don't align?

I believe we can.
But only if we listen more than we label.
And only if we care more about understanding than winning.

What do you think?

How do you stay grounded in your values when conversations get polarized?

Part VI: Philosophy and Life's Big Questions

Some questions don't come with neat answers. But they're still worth asking. In this section, I explore happiness, time, and perspective—not to resolve them but to hold them up to the light. Because meaning isn't always found in certainty. Sometimes it lives in the asking.

Essay 17: The Nature of Happiness

We chase happiness like it's a destination.
A milestone we'll reach once the job is right, the account is full, or the calendar is clear.

I've done it. I've set goals and achieved them, and I still felt the quiet question whispering behind the applause: *Is this it?*

Happiness, I've learned, is not what I thought it was.

It's not constant.
It's not earned through sheer will.
And it doesn't come from getting everything right.

In fact, the times when I've felt most at peace were rarely the times when I had the most success—they were the times when I was most *present*.

But for years, I didn't know how to feel that peace—because I didn't believe I deserved it.

My childhood was unstable, filled with grief, trauma, and loss. As I got older and my life grew more stable, I stubbornly clung to the past. It was like carrying around a bag of bricks—everywhere I went, I dragged it with me. Some part of me believed that happiness would make me forget what I'd survived. So I resisted it. I wore my suffering like a scar that needed to be visible, even when no one was looking.

I convinced myself that the better things got, the more likely they were to fall apart. That disaster was inevitable. That peace was a setup. That joy was just the prelude to loss.

It was, in hindsight, a ridiculous way to live.
But at the time, it made perfect sense.

Every few years, it felt like I was having a midlife crisis—grappling with the same internal battles under a new disguise. And if the people in my life didn't accept that part of me, I'd push them away. Not because they were wrong but because I had built an identity around being misunderstood—and letting go of that meant facing the possibility that maybe, just maybe, happiness wasn't the enemy.

It took time. Growth. Reflection. Some painful honesty. And a long, emotional standoff with my own inner child—who refused to let go of the idea that I had to *hurt* to be real.

But eventually, I realized something that changed everything:

I used to think happiness meant freedom from struggle.
Now I see it's often found *through* struggle.

Not because pain is noble, but because clarity tends to arrive in the quiet that follows hardship. You find yourself stripped of distractions, humbled by experience, and—if you're lucky—more grateful for what remains.

The nature of happiness isn't in what you own.
It's in what you notice.

It's in knowing who you are when no one's watching.
It's in making peace with your past, and having hope for your future.

Vega – Fool for Thought

It's in laughing with your family at dinner after a long,
imperfect day.

That's the hard part: Happiness hides in plain sight.
You don't achieve it. You practice it.

Sometimes it's a deliberate pause.
A deep breath before the meeting.
A decision to walk away from the argument.
Other times, it's subtly embedded in the rhythm of an
ordinary moment.

I no longer think of happiness as a goal.
Some days, it's just a deep breath.
Being at a table with people you love.

A moment of stillness that doesn't ask you to earn it.
You don't chase it.

You notice it.

Sit with this:

*What moment of happiness surprised you by showing up in
the middle of ordinary life?*

Essay 18: Time and the Illusion of Control

I used to treat time like a puzzle I could solve.
If I planned carefully enough, scheduled tightly enough, and stayed just one step ahead, I could control the outcome. I didn't think of it as being controlling, I called it "being prepared."

But life has a way of undoing your most carefully laid plans.

A fall. A diagnosis. A phone call in the middle of the night. These moments don't care about your calendar. They don't check your to-do list. They arrive uninvited and rewrite the script.

That truth hit home in 2023 when I lost my brother, Daniel.

Just a year earlier, we had begun planning to work together—finally—after decades of dreaming about it. I had co-founded Rockwall Capital Group with my wife, Alicia, and the plan was simple: Once the business found its footing, Daniel would join us as VP of operations. It was the perfect fit. He had deep operational expertise, and we shared a vision that extended beyond business—it was personal, redemptive, and rooted in the kind of bond that only siblings who have survived real loss can understand.

We were ready to build something together.
But time had other plans.

Just days after we celebrated at a family wedding in San Antonio, Texas—where Daniel was beaming as he told friends and relatives about our upcoming collaboration—he was gone. May 8, 2023. A day I'll never forget. A dream cut short without warning.

We'd walked different paths in adulthood—me in financial services, him in retail leadership—but we always believed we would meet in the middle. That we could intertwine our professional lives the way we had our personal ones. We had already done the hard work: We had endured childhood loss, navigated fatherlessness, and faced down our own demons. We didn't dwell in victimhood—we moved forward. And this business was meant to be a celebration of all that.

But life doesn't honor perfect timing.
It doesn't wait for dreams to align.
It just … moves. Unapologetically.

And that's when the illusion shatters: We don't control time. We move through it. And if we're not careful, it moves right past us while we're busy trying to master it.

I still struggle with that. I still ask why, even though no answer comes. I still catch myself reaching for a future that no longer exists—and then slowly, painfully, I remember: *This* is the time I have.

This isn't to say planning is pointless. I still believe in goals, discipline, and preparation. But I've learned that the danger comes when we mistake planning for control—when we start believing we can engineer certainty out of uncertainty.

The truth is that time doesn't owe us anything.
It won't slow down when we need a break or speed up when

we're stuck.
It keeps moving—indifferent, consistent, and precious.

So the question becomes: How do we live well inside of
something we can't control?

For me, it starts with humility.
Recognizing that I'm not in charge of the clock.
Then with presence—choosing to show up for the moment
I'm in, not just the one I'm planning for.

Daniel's absence is still loud. Some days, the weight of
unfinished dreams is almost unbearable. But I made a
decision: I will carry his spirit with me. In every risk I take.
In every life I try to touch. In every small, steady step
forward.

Time is not a problem to be solved.
It's a companion.
Sometimes generous. Sometimes harsh. Always honest.

We can't control it. But we can honor it.

By paying attention.
By letting go of what we can't fix.
By holding what matters before it slips away.

Because in the end, the illusion of control fades.
But the life we build inside the time we're given, that's what
remains.

Sit with this:

Has life ever interrupted a plan you thought was solid? What did it teach you about control?

Essay 19: The Power of Perspective

It's easy to think our perspective is reality.
After all, it's the one we've lived in our whole lives. It fits. It makes sense. And when something fits, we don't always question it.

But I've learned—sometimes the hard way—that perspective is not truth. It's a lens. One of many. And if you never change lenses, you might spend your whole life looking at a small piece of the world and thinking it's the whole picture.

I didn't grow up with privilege. But I also didn't grow up with a full understanding of how someone else—living just a few blocks away—might experience life in a completely different way. I remember thinking the world was hard for *me* and assuming everyone else had it easier. Later, I learned that's not how empathy works. The pain isn't a competition. And neither is perspective.

Over the years, my viewpoint has been reshaped by unexpected teachers, including the following:

- A colleague who challenged my assumptions with kindness, not accusation

- A child who asked a simple question I couldn't easily answer

- A leader who held a different worldview but listened without needing to win

83

And if I'm honest, my perspective has also changed in solitude. In moments of reflection when the noise faded long enough for uncomfortable thoughts to surface—ones I might have dismissed before, now demanding attention.

That's the thing about growth. It's not always loud. Sometimes it happens when we quietly realize we've been looking through the wrong lens.

I've found that the ability to shift perspectives—especially when it's inconvenient—is one of the most underrated skills a person can develop. It doesn't mean abandoning your beliefs. It means holding them with enough humility to ask, "What if I'm wrong?" or at the very least, "What else might be true?"

In leadership, it's the difference between control and connection.
In relationships, it's the difference between being right and being kind.
In life, it's the difference between judgment and curiosity.

We live in a time when certainty is applauded and nuance is dismissed as weakness. But I believe the opposite is true: Real strength is having the ability to hold tension, to entertain a thought without needing to adopt it, and to see someone else not as a threat but as a window.

Because when you change the way you look at things, the things you look at start to change.

Sit with this:

When has a shift in your perspective changed everything, even if your circumstances stayed the same?

Part VII: Reflection and Legacy

Legacy isn't what we leave behind someday. It's how we live right now. These final essays are about impact—not in terms of scale but in intention. What we value, what we pass on, and how we make others feel—those are the real imprints we leave behind.

Essay 20: What Will Be Your Legacy?

We don't get to choose how people remember us.
But we do get to choose how we live—and that shapes the memory we leave behind.

Legacy used to feel like something reserved for the famous. The wealthy. The ones with buildings named after them or quotes etched into history books. But over time, I've come to see it differently. Legacy isn't about size. It's about substance. It's the residue of your values, left behind in the lives you've touched.

It's the kid who remembers that you believed in them when no one else did.
The employee who found their voice because you created space for it.
The friend who started seeing themselves differently after a quiet conversation over coffee.

Most of the people who shaped me probably don't know they did.
They didn't set out to "leave a legacy." They were just being present. Consistent. Thoughtful. And their example stayed with me—in some cases, long after they left.

I've lived in more than thirty homes across five states and in fifteen cities. In every place—from San Antonio to New Orleans, Dallas to Chicago—I have left a part of myself behind. And more importantly, I've taken some things with me: Perspective. Experience. Relationships that changed me. Each city, and each season, left a mark not just on my résumé but on my character. That motion, that expansion—it's part of my legacy too.

But geography is only part of it.

There's a deeper thread that started early. I grew up on the west side of San Antonio, Texas, where identity was simple: We were all Chicano, or Mexican American, or just *us*. But when we moved to a different neighborhood, I learned that to others, I was something else entirely—a "poor Mexican." I remember a boy putting his arm around my neck and trying to choke the difference out of me. I hadn't done anything wrong. I had simply existed in brown skin, in the wrong part of town, and that was enough.

That moment could've hardened me. And for a while, it did. But over time, it gave me something else—empathy. It taught me to see people as more than the labels that are thrown at them. And it taught me to build bridges where others have built fences.

Still, I've made my share of mistakes. My journey hasn't been a straight line—it started in the fog of loss. I was broke, angry, and reckless. I made decisions I now regret. I hurt people I loved. But I also rebuilt. Slowly, painfully, one choice at a time. I didn't come from success, but I created some. And in doing so, I discovered the quiet resilience that would become the bedrock of how I lead and how I live.

That, too, is part of legacy—not where you start but how you rise.

So I've stopped thinking about legacy as something I'll craft one day in the future. I think about it as something I am creating now. In how I speak to people who can't do anything for me. In how I treat the janitor and the CEO with equal respect.

Because here's the thing: Your legacy is already forming. Not through your résumé but through your ripple effect. Not through the applause but through the quiet, repeated acts of intention.

It's in the values you model.
The courage you share.
The way you make others feel—safe, challenged, and seen.

So the question isn't "Will I leave a legacy?"
You will.
The question is: "What kind?"

And you answer it—not in words but in how you live today.

Pause and reflect:

What do you hope people will remember about you, and how are you living that now?

Essay 21: Living with Intention

Most days don't ask us to be extraordinary.
They ask us to be present.
To choose deliberately.
To remember that even ordinary moments are building
something.

That's what living with intention means to me. Not some
perfect, hyper-disciplined existence—but a posture of
awareness. A willingness to ask, "What kind of person am I
becoming by doing this?"

I've lived unintentionally before—I was rushed, reactive, and
distracted. It's easy to fall into, especially when life gets
loud. But over time, I began to realize: I wasn't just losing
time. I was losing alignment between who I said I was and
how I was actually showing up.

Living with intention doesn't mean having everything
planned.
It just means your choices aren't made on autopilot.
It's deciding to listen instead of interrupt.
To pause before you post.
To say yes for the right reasons—and no for the right ones,
too.

Sometimes it's a poem written for my wife—not for praise
but because she deserves to know, again and again, just how
deeply I admire her. Some may find it overly sentimental. I
find it essential. When I see how she lights up in response to

something I've written for her, I know: This isn't performance. It's presence. It's me living with intention.

Other times it's a note from someone I worked with years ago. They tell me I made a difference—not with grand gestures but by seeing them, mentoring them, and pushing them toward what they could become. And again, I'm reminded: The small things are the big things.

Reflection used to be something I reserved for journals and late-night thoughts. Now it's the compass I use to realign my daily life. It's how I notice what's working, what's draining me, and what needs to change. Reflection isn't separate from intention—it's what makes it possible.

I think often of Michel de Montaigne, the French essayist who wrote, "I do not portray being; I portray passing." That sentiment has stayed with me. I'm not trying to prove I've arrived. I'm just trying to pay attention as I pass through.

Some days I still fall short. I get pulled into distraction. I chase the wrong priorities. But when I return to reflection, I return to myself. Not to a perfect version but to the truest one I can reach.

I've poured time, money, and energy into my community— not out of obligation but because I'm profoundly aware of how much has been given to me. I'll never repay it all. But I consider it a privilege to try.

These days, I try to move more slowly. To ask better questions. To align my calendar with my values, not just my pressures. To live each day with the quiet awareness that how I spend my time is how I'm spending my life.

That's the quiet truth about intentional living: It won't always look impressive from the outside.
But it will feel right on the inside.

It will leave you with fewer regrets, deeper relationships, and the sense that your life is being shaped on purpose, not by default.

And that, I think, is one of the greatest freedoms we can have.

Pause and reflect:

What intention are you carrying into your next season of life?

Epilogue: Thinking as a Practice

Thinking gets a bad rap these days.
We're told to act fast, decide quickly, and keep moving.
Reflection is often seen as indecision.
Slowing down is treated like weakness.

And yet, the most meaningful changes in my life haven't
come from reacting; they've come from thinking. Not just
surface thinking—the kind that circles around old worries—
but deliberate thought. Quiet thought. Curious thought.

Thinking, I've come to believe, isn't a reaction. It's a
discipline. A practice. Something to be cultivated with
intention—like listening, or forgiveness, or courage.

When I take time to think, I see patterns.
I catch myself mid-habit and ask, "Is this still serving me?"
I find clarity that was buried under noise.
And I make decisions that are less about impulse and more
about alignment.

But here's the thing: Thinking isn't glamorous.
It doesn't come with applause.
You don't get points for pausing.

In fact, thinking deeply might cost you.
It might make you slower to judge, harder to categorize, and
unwilling to shout over the noise just to fit in.
But it will also make you wiser. More grounded. More
comfortable in nuance—and more connected to what really
matters.

Vega – Fool for Thought

Thinking is not a destination.
It's a habit. A posture. A willingness to stay open to ideas, to people, and to the possibility that we might change.

I didn't write this book because I've figured it all out.
I wrote it because I haven't—and because that in itself feels worth sharing.

Like Michel de Montaigne, I've tried to offer not answers but *attempts*—essays in the truest sense of the word. Snapshots of questions I'm still living.

In these pages, I've revisited contradictions I once tried to erase.
I've honored friendships that steadied me more than any philosophy.
I've shared memories of grief, quiet moments of joy, and the power of simply paying attention.

If there's a thread that ties it all together, it's this:
I don't think the goal is clarity.
I think it's presence.
Not a polished life, but a practiced one.
One shaped by reflection, forged through impermanence, and guided—however imperfectly—by intention.

So if you've made it this far, I hope you leave not with certainty but with curiosity.
Not with a script but with permission.

To live fully. To love deeply. To ask better questions.
To own your contradictions and let them humanize you instead of haunt you.

Vega – Fool for Thought

There's wisdom in admitting you're still learning.
There's courage in thinking for yourself.

And there's power in walking this road—not with a blueprint
but with an open heart.

So here's to thinking.
To reflecting.
To staying curious when it would be easier to shut down.
To choosing, day by day, to live—not perfectly but
purposefully.

And if I may leave you with one final thought:

Don't be afraid to be a fool—for thought.
That's where wisdom begins.

Acknowledgments

This book began as a whisper—an inner nudge to capture the thoughts that have shaped my life. But it wouldn't have become a reality without the people who encouraged me to give those thoughts a voice.

To my wife, Alicia—your love, patience, and steady presence have been the grounding force in my life. You see me fully, and love me anyway. This book is as much yours as it is mine.

To my children, Luci, Monica, and David—thank you for reminding me every day what matters most. You are my greatest teachers.

To my friends and family, especially those who said, "You should really write a book someday." You may not have known it, but those words planted something lasting.

To the early readers and editors who helped shape this manuscript, thank you for your honesty, encouragement, and time. Your fingerprints are present throughout these pages.

To the great thinkers who lent me their courage—Michel de Montaigne, Viktor Frankl, Adam Smith, and others—your questions gave shape to mine.

And finally, to every reader who chooses to slow down long enough to reflect, I'm grateful we're walking part of this road together.

Appendix A: Ink Left in the Pen

Not everything I wrote fit neatly into the essays you just read. Some ideas came uninvited—too personal, too poetic, or too raw to shape into structure. But I couldn't leave them behind.

What follows is a small collection of fragments—poems, brief reflections, and narrative moments that offer a quieter window into me.

Throughout this book, I've mentioned people who shaped me—my wife, my mother, and my children. These pages include pieces I wrote for them, about them, or because of them.

I share them not as conclusions but as echoes.
Sentences that stayed with me.
Maybe they'll stay with you, too.

She Lives in Me

My mother didn't live long enough to see who I became, but in truth, she never left.

She taught me that if your story is sad enough, people will pity you, but it won't last. Their hearts might ache at first, but unless you rise, their empathy will quietly fade. Sympathy becomes silence. And eventually, silence becomes apathy.

She told me to work like someone was paying me a million dollars to do a great job—even if the task seemed beneath me. Effort matters more than the title. Dignity comes not from the job you have but how you do it. "If you treat it like it's worth a million," she said, "someday it might become something more."

She reminded me I should bow to no one. People will try to make you feel less than—sometimes out of ignorance, sometimes out of cruelty, and sometimes because they need you to be small so they can feel big. That's not about you. But you might still become their token. Know that, and rise anyway.

I don't know how good a dad I am. My children are doing well by the world's standards, but time will be the truest measure. Still, if I've given them even a shadow of what my mom gave me—strength, pride, and hope—I will have lived a good life.

She lives in me. And I hope, through me, she lives in them.

For Alicia

You see the version of me I sometimes forget to be.
And somehow, you love both.

Endlessly True

Every dawn, our light endears
Sweet whispers, over the years
Myriad moments, no love undone
Endlessly you, my true and one

Vega – Fool for Thought

Laughter lingers, melody sweet
Songs of love our hearts repeat
Past nor future dims this flame
Time itself can't break this claim

In union, the world stands still
Heartbeat echoes by pure will
Thousand stars line the night
None outshine your soul's light

Here we stand as love remains
Boundless joys; softened pains
This Valentine's, as ever before
I love you, deeply—forevermore

Fatherhood Changed Everything

There was a time when I thought success was the top of the mountain.
Now I think it's carrying someone else up with you.

Nothing prepared me for fatherhood. And everything prepared me for it.

I have never felt more uncertain—or more clear.
I thought I knew what mattered. I was wrong.
I thought I had loved deeply. I hadn't.

Vega – Fool for Thought

Fatherhood rearranged me.
It asked for more than I thought I had—and then gave it back
in ways I didn't know I needed.

A Life Examined: On Contradictions

My life is a long list of contradictions.

I never made it past the ninth grade. But years later, I
graduated from college with honors. I came from nothing—
not because I was lacking but because my childhood worked
against me. When I should have fought, I gave up. And when
I finally stood up, it was because I had no other choice—and
a lot of help.

At seventeen, no one would have bet on me. Not to be happy.
Not to be whole. Not to succeed.

And yet, here I am.

Like Michel de Montaigne, I've always suffered from never
feeling like I had enough. He came from royalty. I came from
a broken place. But we shared the same curse—and the same
power: reflection.

He lived over five hundred years ago. But based on his
legacy, I'd like to think he died knowing it was, in fact, a
good life.

And I believe I have, too.

For Frank

Some people step into your life quietly—and hold it together without fanfare. Frank was that person for me.

I come from a large family—one of seven children. When people ask where I fall in the lineup, I tell them: right in the middle. Each of my siblings played a different role—some as confidants, others as protectors or challengers. But one person stands above the rest: my eldest brother, Frank.

When our mother passed away, my younger siblings and I were suddenly orphaned. We each went to live with different relatives, but I bounced around until I ended up with Frank. And here's the thing: I wasn't the only one. Every one of my younger siblings spent meaningful time in Frank's home.

Frank was a young husband and father himself, living in a modest three-bedroom house on the west side of San Antonio, Texas. He didn't have much, but he had something more powerful than resources: resolve. He believed that family came first. And no matter how difficult or ungrateful we were—and trust me, we tested him—he never turned us away.

He supported us. Challenged us. Believed in us. And did it all without asking for thanks.

I've told him before how much that meant to me, and every time, he shrugs it off like it was nothing. But I know better. Without Frank's steadiness and strength, my life might have taken a very different path.

I like to think my mother would be proud of the man I've become. But I'll always stand in the shadow of my big brother—the man who chose to carry others when he could have walked away.

Lucky

People call me lucky, but they don't know how many times I've failed just to get here.

Open Heart, Mind Will Follow

When your heart opens, your mind doesn't just follow—it expands.

Appendix B: Books That Shaped My Thinking

I didn't come to books through academia. I came to them through necessity. I needed new ways to think, better questions to ask, and reminders that my story wasn't finished. The books listed here didn't hand me answers— they gave me frameworks, challenges, and a few necessary disruptions.

Predictably Irrational by **Dan Ariely**
This one is funny, surprising, and unsettling in the best way. It revealed just how flawed we are—and how understanding those flaws can make us more generous.

Against the Gods by **Peter Bernstein**
This is a masterful telling of how humans came to understand risk. It changed how I view uncertainty—not as something to fear but as something to measure.

Origin Story: A Big History of Everything by **David Christian**
This book zoomed out farther than any other I've read. A reminder that we're small, but also part of something staggeringly vast and interconnected.

A Brief History of Thought by **Luc Ferry**
A deceptively small book with enormous ideas. It helped me see philosophy not as abstraction but as a human response to life's deepest questions.

Thinking, Fast and Slow by **Daniel Kahneman**

This book reshaped how I process decisions, especially when I'm under pressure. It helped me see that thinking isn't just what we do—it's how we do everything.

***The Better Angels of Our Nature* by Steven Pinker**
This is not a feel-good book, but one that gave me hope. A long view of human progress that reminded me why it's worth caring, even when the headlines say otherwise.

***The Blank Slate* by Steven Pinker**
This book challenged my assumptions about nature, nurture, and identity. Whether or not I agreed with every point, it sharpened my thinking.

***The Four Agreements* by Don Miguel Ruiz**
A short book, but one that rattled me. It offered clarity when my mind was cluttered, and it helped me reframe how I manage expectations—both mine and others'.

***The Genius in All of Us* by David Shenk**
I've always been fascinated by potential—and this book affirmed what I've long believed: Talent is nurtured, not born.

***The Theory of Moral Sentiments* by Adam Smith**
Everyone quotes *Wealth of Nations*, but this one shows his heart. It reminded me that economic life is still human life—and sympathy, not self-interest, may be our deepest driver.

***The Wealth of Nations* by Adam Smith**
More than a book about economics—it's a window into incentives, systems, and how human behavior responds to structure. Still relevant, still revelatory.

Educated by Tara Westover

This one cut deep. It reminded me that education is more than access—it's escape, it's identity, and it's survival. A haunting and hopeful story.

Bibliography

Bakewell, S. *How to Live: Or a Life of Montaigne in One Question and Twenty Attempts at an Answer*. Other Press, 2010.

Descartes, R. *Discourse on the Method*. Translated by I. Maclean. Oxford University Press, 2006.

Frankl, V. E. *Man's Search for Meaning*. Beacon Press, 2006.

Henley, W. E. "Invictus." In *The Oxford Book of English Verse*, edited by J. W. Day. Oxford University Press, 1900.

Kahneman, D. *Thinking, Fast and Slow*. Farrar, Straus and Giroux, 2011.

Montaigne, M. de. *The Complete Essays*. Translated by M. A. Screech. Penguin Books, 1993.

Richman, I. B. *The Spanish Conquerors*. Macmillan, 1907.

Smith, A. *The Theory of Moral Sentiments*. Edited by K. Haakonssen. Cambridge University Press, 2002.

About the Author

David Vega is a writer, business leader, and community advocate who believes in the quiet power of reflection. With a career spanning executive leadership, entrepreneurship, and nonprofit service, David brings a unique blend of real-world experience and philosophical depth to his work.

He is the founder and CEO of Rockwall Capital Group, a private equity and consulting firm that acquired *The Rockwall Times* to support small business growth through thoughtful journalism and local storytelling. Prior to launching his own ventures, David held senior leadership roles in the insurance and financial services industries, where he was known for his integrity, empathy, and ability to bridge strategy with heart.

But titles don't tell the whole story.

A first-generation college graduate who overcame early hardship, David writes not from the mountaintop but from the trail—still walking, still learning. *Fool for Thought* is his first book, born out of gratitude for the people, questions, and contradictions that shaped him.

He lives in Texas with his wife and son, where he continues to write, mentor, and find joy in meaningful conversation.

For updates and bonus content, or to get in touch, visit https://www.foolforthought.life.

www.ingramcontent.com/pod-product-compliance
Lightning Source LLC
Chambersburg PA
CBHW070345130626
46556CB00007B/3037